Feminism for
the 99 Percent

Feminism for the 99 Percent

A Manifesto

Cinzia Arruzza
Tithi Bhattacharya
Nancy Fraser

VERSO
London • New York

First published by Verso 2019
© Cinzia Arruzza, Tithi Bhattacharya, Nancy Fraser 2019

The moral rights of the authors have been asserted

7 9 10 8 6

Verso
UK: 6 Meard Street, London W1F 0EG
US: 20 Jay Street, Suite 1010, Brooklyn, NY 11201
versobooks.com

Verso is the imprint of New Left Books

ISBN-13: 978-1-78873-442-4
ISBN-13: 978-1-78873-444-8 (UK EBK)
ISBN-13: 978-1-78873-445-5 (US EBK)

British Library Cataloguing in Publication Data
A catalogue record for this book is available from the British Library

Library of Congress Cataloging-in-Publication Data
A catalog record for this book is available from the Library of Congress

Typeset in Sabon by Hewer Text UK Ltd, Edinburgh
Printed and bound by CPI Group (UK) Ltd, Croydon, CR0 4YY

For the Combahee River Collective,
who envisioned the path early on

and for the Polish and Argentine feminist strikers,
who are breaking new ground today

Contents

A Manifesto

A fork in the road

In the spring of 2018, Facebook COO Sheryl Sandberg told the world that we "would be a lot better off if half of all countries and companies were run by women and half of all homes were run by men," and that "we shouldn't be satisfied until we reach that goal." A leading exponent of corporate feminism, Sandberg had already made a name (and a buck) for herself by urging women managers to "lean in" at the company boardroom. As former chief of staff to US Treasury Secretary Larry Summers—the man who deregulated Wall Street—she had no qualms about counseling women that success won through toughness in the business world was the royal road to gender equality.

That same spring, a militant feminist strike shut down Spain. Joined by more than 5 million marchers, organizers of the twenty-four-hour *huelga feminista* called for "a society free of sexist oppression, exploitation and violence . . . for rebellion and a struggle against the alliance of the patriarchy and capitalism that wants us to be obedient, submissive and quiet." As the sun set over Madrid and Barcelona, the feminist strikers announced to the world, "On March 8 we cross our arms, interrupt[ing] all productive and reproductive activity," declaring they would not "accept worse working conditions, nor being paid less than men for the same work."

These two voices represent opposing paths for the feminist movement. On the one hand, Sandberg and her ilk see feminism as a handmaiden of capitalism. They want a world where the task of managing exploitation in the workplace and oppression in the social whole is shared equally by ruling-class men and women. This is a remarkable vision of *equal opportunity domination*: one that asks ordinary people, in the name of feminism, to be grateful that it is a woman, not a man, who busts their union, orders a drone to kill their parent, or locks their child in a cage at the border. In sharp contrast to Sandberg's liberal feminism, the organizers of the *huelga feminista* insist on *ending capitalism*: the system that generates the boss, produces national borders, and manufactures the drones that guard them.

Faced with these two visions of feminism, we find ourselves at a fork in the road, and our choice bears extraordinary consequences for humankind. One path leads to a scorched planet where human life is immiserated to the point of unrecognizability, if indeed it remains possible at all. The other points to the sort of world that has always figured centrally in humanity's most exalted dreams: a just world whose wealth and natural resources are shared by all, and where equality and freedom are premises, not aspirations.

The contrast could not be starker. But what makes the choice pressing for us now is the absence of any viable middle way. We owe the dearth of alternatives to neoliberalism: that exceptionally predatory, financialized form of capitalism that has held sway across the globe for the last forty years. Having poisoned the atmosphere, mocked every pretense of democratic rule, stretched our social capacities to their breaking point, and worsened living conditions generally for the vast majority, this iteration of capitalism has raised the stakes for every social struggle, transforming sober efforts to win modest reforms into pitched battles for survival. Under such conditions, the time for fence-sitting is past, and feminists must take a stand: Will we continue to pursue "equal opportunity domination" while the planet burns? Or will we reimagine gender justice in an anticapitalist form—one that leads beyond the present crisis to a new society?

This manifesto is a brief for the second path, a course we deem both necessary and feasible. An anticapitalist feminism has become thinkable today, in part because the credibility of political elites is collapsing worldwide. The casualties include not only the center-left and center-right parties that promoted neoliberalism—now despised remnants of their former selves—but also their Sandberg-style corporate feminist allies, whose "progressive" veneer has lost its shine. Liberal feminism met its waterloo in the US presidential election of 2016, when the much-ballyhooed candidacy of Hillary Clinton failed to excite women voters. And for good reason: Clinton personified the deepening disconnect between elite women's ascension to high office and improvements in the lives of the vast majority.

Clinton's defeat is our wake-up call. Exposing the bankruptcy of liberal feminism, it has created an opening for a challenge to it from the left. In the vacuum produced by liberalism's decline, we have a chance to build another feminism: a feminism with a different definition of what counts as a feminist issue, a different class orientation, and a different ethos—one that is radical and transformative.

This manifesto is our effort to promote that "other" feminism. We write not to sketch an imagined utopia, but to mark out the road that must be traveled to reach a just society. We aim to explain why feminists should choose the road of feminist strikes, why we must unite with other anticapitalist and antisystemic movements, and why our movement must become a *feminism for the 99 percent*. Only in this way—by connecting with antiracists, environmentalists, and labor and migrant rights activists—can feminism rise to the challenge of our times. By decisively rejecting "lean in" dogma and the feminism of the 1 percent, *our* feminism can become a beacon of hope for everyone else.

What gives us the courage to embark on this project now is the new wave of militant feminist activism. This is not the corporate feminism that has proved so disastrous for working women and is now hemorrhaging credibility; nor is it the "microcredit feminism" that claims to "empower" women of the global South by lending them tiny sums of money. Rather, what give us hope are the international feminist and women's strikes of 2017 and 2018. It is these strikes, and the increasingly coordinated movements that are developing around them, that first inspired—and now embody—a feminism for the 99 percent.

Thesis 1: A new feminist wave is reinventing the strike.

The recent feminist strike movement began in Poland in October of 2016, when more than 100,000 women staged walkouts and marches to oppose the country's ban on abortion. By the end of the month, an upwelling of radical refusal had already crossed the ocean to Argentina, where striking women met the heinous murder of Lucía Pérez with the militant cry: "Ni una menos." Soon it spread to Italy, Spain, Brazil, Turkey, Peru, the United States, Mexico, Chile, and dozens of other countries. From its origins in the streets, the movement then surged through workplaces and schools, eventually engulfing the high-flying worlds of show business, media, and politics. For the last two years, its slogans have resonated powerfully across the globe: #NosotrasParamos, #WeStrike, #VivasNosQueremos, #NiUnaMenos, #TimesUp, #Feminism4the99. At first a ripple, then a wave, it has become a massive tide: a new global feminist movement that may gain sufficient force to disrupt existing alliances and redraw the political map.

What had been a series of nationally based actions became a transnational movement on March 8, 2017, when organizers around the globe decided to strike together. With this bold stroke, they re-politicized International Women's Day. Brushing aside the tacky baubles of depoliticization—brunches, mimosas, and Hallmark cards—the strikers have revived the day's all-but-forgotten historical roots in working-class and socialist feminism. Their actions evoke the spirit of early twentieth century working class women's mobilization—paradigmatically the strikes and mass demonstrations led mostly by immigrant and Jewish women in the United States, which inspired US socialists to organize the first National Women's Day and German socialists Luise Zietz and Clara Zetkin to call for an International Working Women's Day.

Re-animating that militant spirit, the feminist strikes of today are reclaiming our roots in historic struggles for workers' rights and social justice. Uniting women separated by oceans, mountains, and continents, as well as by borders, barbed wire fences, and walls, they give new meaning to the slogan "Solidarity is our weapon." Breaking through the isolation of domestic and symbolic walls, the strikes demonstrate the enormous political potential of women's power: *the power of those whose paid and unpaid work sustains the world*.

But that is not all: this burgeoning movement has

invented *new ways to strike* and infused the strike form itself with a *new kind of politics*. By coupling the withdrawal of labor with marches, demon-strations, small business closures, blockades, and boycotts, the movement is replenishing the repertoire of strike actions, once large but dramatically shrunk by a decades-long neoliberal offensive. At the same time, this new wave is democratizing strikes and expanding their scope—above all, by broadening the very idea of what counts as "labor." Refusing to limit that category to waged work, women's strike activism is also withdrawing housework, sex, and smiles. By making visible *the indispensable role played by gendered, unpaid work in capitalist society*, it draws attention to activities from which capital benefits, but for which it does not pay. And with respect to paid work, too, the strikers take an expansive view of what counts as a labor issue. Far from focusing only on wages and hours, they are also targeting sexual harassment and assault, barriers to reproductive justice, and curbs on the right to strike.

As a result, the new feminist wave has the potential to overcome the stubborn and divisive opposition between "identity politics" and "class politics." Disclosing the unity of "workplace" and "private life," it refuses to limit its struggles to those spaces. And by redefining what counts as "work" and who counts as a "worker," it rejects capitalism's structural undervaluation of women's labor—both paid and unpaid. All told, women's strike feminism anticipates the possibility of a new, unprecedented phase of class struggle: feminist, internationalist, environmentalist, and anti-racist.

This intervention is perfectly timed. Women's strike militancy has erupted at a moment when once-powerful trade unions, centered in manufacturing, have been severely weakened. To reinvigorate class struggle, activists have turned to another arena: the neoliberal assault on health care, education, pensions, and housing. In targeting this other prong of capital's four-decade attack on working- and middle-class living conditions, they have trained their sights on the labor and services that are needed to sustain human beings and social communities. It is here, in the sphere of "social reproduction," that we now find many of the most militant strikes and fightbacks. From the strike wave of teachers in the United States to the struggle against water privatization in Ireland to the strikes of Dalit sanitation workers in India—all led and powered by women—workers are revolting against capital's assault on social reproduction. Although not formally affiliated with the International Women's Strike movement, these strikes have much in common with it. They, too, valorize the work that is necessary to reproduce our lives, while opposing its exploitation; and they, too, combine wage and workplace demands with demands for increased public spending on social services.

In countries such as Argentina, Spain, and Italy, moreover, women's strike feminism has attracted broad support from forces opposing austerity. Not only women and gender-nonconforming people, but also men have joined the movement's massive demonstrations against the defunding of schools, health care, housing, transport, and environmental protections. Through their opposition to finance capital's assault on these "public goods," feminist strikes are thus becoming the catalyst and model for broad-based efforts to defend our communities.

All told, the new wave of militant feminist activism is rediscovering the idea of the impossible, demanding both bread and roses: the bread that decades of neoliberalism have taken from our tables, but also the beauty that nourishes our spirit through the exhilaration of rebellion.

Thesis 2: Liberal feminism is bankrupt. It's time to get over it.

The mainstream media continues to equate *feminism*, as such, with *liberal feminism*. But far from providing the solution, liberal feminism is part of the problem. Centered in the global North among the professional-managerial stratum, it is focused on "leaning-in" and "cracking the glass ceiling." Dedicated to enabling a smattering of privileged women to climb the corporate ladder and the ranks of the military, it propounds a market-centered view of equality that dovetails perfectly with the prevailing corporate enthusiasm for "diversity." Although it condemns "discrimination" and advocates "freedom of choice," liberal feminism steadfastly refuses to address the socioeconomic constraints that make freedom and empowerment impossible for the large majority of women. Its real aim is not equality, but meritocracy. Rather than seeking to abolish social hierarchy, it aims to "diversify" it, "empowering" "talented" women to rise to the top. In treating women simply as an "underrepresented group," its proponents seek to ensure that a few privileged souls can attain positions and pay on a par with the men *of their own class*. By definition, the principal beneficiaries are those who already possess considerable social, cultural, and economic advantages. Everyone else remains stuck in the basement.

Fully compatible with ballooning inequality, liberal feminism outsources oppression. It permits professional-managerial women to *lean in* precisely by enabling them to *lean on* the poorly paid migrant women to whom they subcontract their caregiving and housework. Insensitive to class and race, it links our cause with elitism and individualism. Projecting feminism as a "stand-alone" movement, it associates us with policies that harm the majority and cuts us off from struggles that oppose those policies. In short, liberal feminism gives feminism a bad name.

Liberal feminism's ethos converges not only with corporate mores but also with supposedly "transgressive" currents of neoliberal culture. Its love affair with individual advancement equally permeates the world of social-media celebrity, which also confuses feminism with the ascent of individual women. In that world, "feminism" risks becoming a trending hashtag and a vehicle of self-promotion, deployed less to liberate the many than to elevate the few.

In general, then, liberal feminism supplies the perfect alibi for neoliberalism. Cloaking regressive policies in an aura of emancipation, it enables the forces supporting global capital to portray themselves as "progressive." Allied with global finance in the United States, while providing cover for Islamophobia in Europe, this is the feminism of the female power-holders: the corporate gurus who preach "lean in," the femocrats who push structural adjustment and microcredit on the global

South, and the professional politicians in pant suits who collect six-figure fees for speeches to Wall Street.

Our answer to *lean-in* feminism is *kick-back* feminism. We have no interest in breaking the glass ceiling while leaving the vast majority to clean up the shards. Far from celebrating women CEOs who occupy corner offices, we want to get rid of CEOs and corner offices.

Thesis 3: We need an anticapitalist feminism—a feminism for the 99 percent.

The feminism we have in mind recognizes that it must respond to a crisis of epochal proportions: plummeting living standards and looming ecological disaster; rampaging wars and intensified dispossession; mass migrations met with barbed wire; emboldened racism and xenophobia; and the reversal of hard-won rights—both social and political.

We aspire to meet these challenges. Eschewing half-measures, the feminism we envision aims to tackle the capitalist roots of metastasizing barbarism. Refusing to sacrifice the well-being of the many in order to protect the freedom of the few, it champions the needs and rights of the many—of poor and working-class women, of racialized and migrant women, of queer, trans, and disabled women, of women encouraged to see themselves as "middle class" even as capital exploits them. But that is not all. This feminism does not limit itself to "women's issues" as they are traditionally defined. Standing for all who are exploited, dominated, and oppressed, it aims to become a source of hope for the whole of humanity. That is why we call it *a feminism for the 99 percent*.

Inspired by the new wave of women's strikes, feminism for the 99 percent is emerging from the crucible of practical experience, as informed by theoretical reflection. As neoliberalism reshapes gender oppression before our eyes, we see that the only way that women and gender non-conforming people can actualize the rights they have on paper or might still win is by transforming the underlying social system that hollows out rights. By itself, legal abortion does little for poor and working-class women who have neither the means to pay for it nor access to clinics that provide it. Rather, reproductive justice requires free, universal, not-for-profit health care, as well as the end of racist, eugenicist practices in the medical profession. Likewise for poor and working-class women, wage equality can mean only equality in misery unless it comes with jobs that pay a generous living wage, with substantive, actionable labor rights, and with a new organization of house- and carework. Then, too, laws criminalizing gender violence are a cruel hoax if they turn a blind eye to the structural sexism and racism of criminal justice systems, leaving intact police brutality, mass incarceration, deportation threats, military interventions, and harassment and abuse in the workplace. Finally, legal emancipation remains an empty shell if it does not include public services, social housing, and funding to ensure that women can leave domestic and workplace violence.

In these ways and more, feminism for the 99 percent seeks profound, far-reaching social transformation. That, in a nutshell, is why it cannot be a separatist movement. We propose, rather, to join with every movement that fights for the 99 percent, whether by struggling for environmental justice, free high-quality education, generous public services, low-cost housing, labor rights, free universal health care, or a world without racism or war. It is only by allying with such movements that we gain the power and vision to dismantle the social relations and the institutions that oppress us.

Feminism for the 99 percent embraces class struggle and the fight against institutional racism. It centers the concerns of working-class women of all stripes: whether racialized, migrant, or white; cis, trans or gender non-conforming; housewives or sex workers; paid by the hour, the week, the month or not at all; unemployed or precarious; young or old. Staunchly internationalist, it is firmly opposed to imperialism and war. *Feminism for the 99 percent is not only antineoliberal, but also anticapitalist.*

Thesis 4: What we are living through is a crisis of society as a whole— and its root cause is capitalism.

For mainstream observers, 2007–2008 marked the beginning of the worst financial crisis since the 1930s. Although correct as far as it goes, that understanding of the present crisis is still too narrow. What we are living through is *a crisis of society as a whole*. By no means restricted to the precincts of finance, it is simultaneously a crisis of economy, ecology, politics, and "care." A general crisis of an entire form of social organization, it is at bottom a crisis of *capitalism*— and in particular, of the viciously predatory form of capitalism we inhabit today: globalizing, financialized, neoliberal.

Capitalism generates such crises periodically— and for reasons that are not accidental. Not only does this system live by exploiting wage labor, it also free-rides on nature, public goods, and the unwaged work that reproduces human beings and communities. Driven by relentless pursuit of unlimited profit, capital expands by helping itself to all of those things without paying for their replacement (except where it is forced to do so). Primed by its very logic to degrade nature, instrumentalize public powers, and commandeer unwaged carework, capital periodically destabilizes the very conditions that it—and the rest of us—rely upon to survive. Crisis is hardwired into its DNA.

Today's crisis of capitalism is especially severe. Four decades of neoliberalism have driven down wages, weakened labor rights, ravaged the environment, and usurped the energies available to sustain families and communities—all while spreading the tentacles of finance across the social fabric. No wonder, then, that masses of people throughout the world are now saying, "*Basta!*" Open to thinking outside the box, they are rejecting established political parties and neoliberal commonsense about "free market competition," "trickle-down economics," "labor market flexibility," and "unsustainable debt." The result is a gaping vacuum of leadership and organization—and a growing sense that something must give.

Feminism for the 99 percent is among the social forces that have leapt into this breach. We do not, however, command the terrain. Rather, we share the stage with many bad actors. Upstart right-wing movements everywhere promise to improve the lot of families of "the right" ethnicity, nationality and religion by ending "free trade," curtailing immigration, and restricting the rights of women, people of color, and LGBTQ+ people. Meanwhile, on the other side, dominant currents of "the progressive resistance" advance an equally unsavory agenda. In their efforts to restore the status quo ante, partisans of global finance hope to convince feminists, anti-racists, and environmentalists to close ranks with their liberal "protectors" and to forego more ambitious, egalitarian projects of social transformation. Feminists for the 99 percent decline that proposal. Rejecting not only reactionary populism but also its progressive neoliberal opponents, *we intend to identify, and confront head on, the real source of crisis and misery, which is capitalism.*

For us, in other words, a crisis is not simply a time of suffering—still less a mere impasse in profit-making. Crucially, it is also a moment of political awakening and an opportunity for social transformation. In times of crisis, critical masses of people withdraw their support from the powers that be. Rejecting politics as usual, they begin to search for new ideas, organizations, and alliances. In such situations, the burning questions are, who will guide the process of societal transformation, in whose interest, and to what end?

This type of process, whereby general crisis leads to societal reorganization, has played out several times in modern history—largely to capital's benefit. Seeking to restore profitability, its champions have reinvented capitalism time and again—reconfiguring not only the official economy, but also politics, social reproduction, and our relation to nonhuman nature. In so doing, they have reorganized not only class exploitation, but also gender and racial oppression, often appropriating rebellious energies (including feminist energies) for projects that over-whelmingly benefit the 1 percent.

Will this process be repeated today? Historically, the 1 percent have always been indifferent to the interests of society or the majority. But today they are especially dangerous. In their single-minded pursuit of short-term profits, they fail to gauge not only the depth of the crisis, but also the threat it poses to the long-term health of the capitalist system itself: they would rather drill for oil now than ensure the ecological preconditions for their own future profits!

As a result, the crisis we confront threatens *life as we know it*. The struggle to resolve it poses the most fundamental questions of social organization: Where will we draw the line delimiting economy from society, society from nature, production from reproduction, and work from family? How will we use the social surplus we collectively produce? And who, exactly, will decide these matters? Will profit-makers manage to turn capitalism's social contradictions into new opportunities for accumulating private wealth? Will they co-opt important strands of feminist rebellion, even as they reorganize gender hierarchy? Or will a mass uprising against capital finally be "the act by which the human race travelling in the [runaway] train applies the emergency brake"? And if so, will feminists be at the forefront of that uprising?

If we have any say in this matter, the answer to the last question will be *yes*.

Thesis 5: Gender oppression in capitalist societies is rooted in the subordination of social reproduction to production for profit. We want to turn things right side up.

Many people know that capitalist societies are by definition class societies, which license a small minority to accumulate private profits by exploiting the much larger group who must work for wages. What is less widely understood is that *capitalist societies are also by definition wellsprings of gender oppression.* Far from being accidental, sexism is hardwired into their very structure.

Certainly, capitalism did not invent the subordination of women. The latter existed in various forms in all previous class societies. But capitalism established new, distinctively "modern" forms of sexism, underpinned by new institutional structures. *Its key move was to separate the making of people from the making of profit, to assign the first job to women, and to subordinate it to the second.* With this stroke, capitalism simultaneously reinvented women's oppression and turned the whole world upside down.

The perversity becomes clear when we recall how vital and complex the work of people-making actually is. Not only does this activity create and sustain life in the biological sense; it also creates and sustains our capacity to work—or what Marx called our "labor power." And that means fashioning people with the "right" attitudes, dispositions, and values—abilities, competences, and skills. All told, people-making work supplies some fundamental preconditions—material, social, cultural—for human society in general and for capitalist production in particular. Without it neither life nor labor power could be embodied in human beings.

We call this vast body of vital activity *social reproduction.*

In capitalist societies, the pivotally important role of social reproduction is disguised and disavowed. Far from being valued in its own right, the making of people is treated as a mere means to the making of profit. Because capital avoids paying for this work to the extent that it can, while treating money as the be-all and end-all, it relegates those who perform social-reproductive labor to a position of subordination—not only to the owners of capital, but also to those more advantaged waged workers who can offload the responsibility for it onto others.

Those "others" are largely female. For in capitalist society, *the organization of social reproduction rests on gender: it relies on gender roles and entrenches gender oppression.* Social reproduction is therefore a feminist issue. But it is shot through at every point by the fault lines of class, race, sexuality, and nation. A feminism aimed at resolving the current crisis must understand social reproduction through a lens that also comprehends, and connects, all those axes of domination.

Capitalist societies have always instituted a racial division of reproductive labor. Whether via slavery or colonialism, apartheid or neo-imperialism, this system has coerced racialized women to provide such labor gratis—or at a very low cost—for their majority-ethnicity or white "sisters." Forced to lavish care on the children and homes of their mistresses or employers, they have had to struggle all the harder to care for their own. Historically, moreover, capitalist societies have sought to enlist women's social reproductive work in the service of gender binarism and heteronormativity. They have encouraged mothers, teachers, and doctors, among others, to ensure that children are strictly fashioned as cis-girls or cis-boys and as heterosexuals. Then, too, modern states have often tried to instrumentalize the work of people-making for national and imperial projects. Incentivizing births of the "right" kind, while discouraging those of the "wrong" kind, they have designed education and family policies to produce not just "people" but (for example) "Germans," "Italians," or "Americans" who can be called on to sacrifice for the nation when needed. Finally, the class character of social reproduction is fundamental. Working-class mothers and schools have been expected to prepare their kids for lives as proper "workers": obedient, deferential to bosses, and primed to accept "their station" and tolerate exploitation. These pressures have never worked perfectly, and even misfired spectacularly on occasion. And some of them are lessening today. But social reproduction is deeply entangled with domination—and with the struggle against it.

Once we understand the centrality of social reproduction in capitalist society, we can no longer view class in the usual way. Contra old-school understandings, what makes class in capitalist society are not just relations that directly exploit "labor" but also relations that produce and replenish it. Nor is the global working class comprised exclusively of those who work for wages in factories or mines. Equally central are those who work in the fields and in private homes; in offices, hotels, and restaurants; in hospitals, nurseries, and schools; in the public sector and in civil society—the precariat, the unemployed, and those who receive no pay in return for their work. Far from being restricted to straight white men, in whose image it is still too often imagined, the bulk of the global working class is made up of migrants, racialized people, women—both cis and trans—and people with different abilities, all of whose needs and desires are negated or twisted by capitalism.

This lens also expands our view of class struggle. Not focused exclusively on economic gains in the workplace like fair contracts or the minimum wage, it occurs at multiple sites in society and not only through unions and official workers' organizations. The critical point for us, and the key to understanding the present, is that *class struggle includes struggles over social reproduction*: for universal health care and free education, for environmental justice and access to clean energy, and for housing and public transportation. Equally central to it are political struggles for women's liberation, against racism and xenophobia, war and colonialism.

Such conflicts have always been central to capitalist society, which relies on reproductive labor while disavowing its value. But social reproduction struggles are especially explosive today. As neoliberalism demands more hours of waged work per household and less state support for social welfare, it squeezes families, communities, and (above all) women to the breaking point. Under these conditions of universal expropriation, struggles over social reproduction have taken center stage. They now form the leading edge of projects with the potential to alter society, root and branch.

Thesis 6: Gender violence takes many forms, all of them entangled with capitalist social relations. We vow to fight them all.

Researchers estimate that, globally, more than one in three women have experienced some form of gender violence in the course of their lifetimes. Many of the perpetrators are intimate partners, responsible for a whopping 38 percent of the murders of women. Liable to be physical, emotional, sexual, or all of the above, intimate partner violence is found throughout capitalist society—in every nation, class, and racial-ethnic group. *Far from being accidental, it is grounded in the basic institutional structure of capitalist society.*

The gender violence we experience today reflects the contradictory dynamics of family and personal life in capitalist society. And these in turn are based in the system's signature division between people-making and profit-making, family and "work." A key development was the shift from the extended kin-based households of an earlier time—in which male elders held the power of life and death over their dependents—to the restricted, heterosexual nuclear family of capitalist modernity, which vested an attenuated right of rule in the "smaller" men who headed smaller households. With this shift, the character of kin-based gender violence was trans-figured. What was once overtly political now became "private": more informal and "psychologi-cal," less "rational" and *controlled*. Often fueled by alcohol, shame, and anxiety about maintaining dominance, this sort of gender violence is found in every period of capitalist development. Nevertheless, it becomes especially virulent and pervasive in times of crisis. In such times, when status anxiety, economic precarity, and political uncertainty loom large, the gender order, too, appears to tremble.

Some men experience women as "out of control," and modern society, with its new sexual freedoms and gender fluidity, as "out of joint." Their wives or girlfriends are "uppity," their homes "disordered," and their children "wild." Their bosses are unrelenting, their coworkers unjustly favored, and their jobs at risk. Their sexual prowess and powers of seduction are in doubt. Perceiving their masculinity to be threatened, they explode.

But not all gender violence in capitalist society takes this apparently "private," "irrational" form. Other types are all too "rational": witness the instrumentalization of gendered assault as a technique of control. Examples include the widespread weaponization of the rape of enslaved and colonized women to terrorize communities of color and enforce their subjugation; the repeated rape of women by pimps and traffickers to "break them in"; and the coordinated mass rape of "enemy" women as a weapon of war. Often instrumental, too, are sexual assault and harassment in workplaces, schools, or clinics. In these cases, the perpetrators are bosses and supervisors, teachers and coaches, policemen and prison guards, doctors and shrinks, landlords and army officers—all with public institutional power over those on whom they prey. They *can* command sexual services, and so some of them do. Here, the root is women's economic, professional, political, and racial vulnerability: our dependence on the paycheck, the reference, the willingness of the employer or foreman not to ask about immigration status. What enables this violence is a system of hierarchical power that fuses gender, race, and class. What results from it is that system's reinforcement and normalization.

In fact, these two forms of gender violence—one private, the other public—are not so separate, after all. There exist hybrid cases, such as teenage, fraternity, and athletic subcultures in which young men, channeling institutionalized misogyny, vie with each other for status and bragging rights by abusing women. Moreover, some forms of public and private gender violence form a mutually reinforcing vicious cycle. Because capitalism assigns reproductive work overwhelmingly to women, it restricts our ability to participate fully, as peers, in the world of "productive work," with the result that most of us land in dead-end jobs that don't pay enough to support a family. That rebounds on "private" life to our disadvantage, as our lesser ability to exit relationships disempowers us within them. The primary beneficiary of the overall arrangement is capital, to be sure. But its effect is to render us doubly subject to violation—first at the hands of familial and personal intimates, and second at those of capital's enforcers and enablers.

The conventional feminist responses to gender violence are understandable, but nonetheless inadequate. The most widespread response is the demand for criminalization and punishment. This "carceral feminism," as it has been called, takes for granted precisely what needs to be called into question: the mistaken assumption that the laws, police, and courts maintain sufficient autonomy from the capitalist power structure to counter its deep-seated tendency to generate gender violence. In fact, the criminal justice system disproportionately targets poor and working-class men of color, including migrants, while leaving their white-collar professional counterparts free to rape and batter; it also leaves women to pick up the pieces: traveling long distances to visit incarcerated sons and husbands, providing for their households alone, and dealing with the legal and bureaucratic fall-out of imprisonment. Likewise, anti-trafficking campaigns and laws against "sexual slavery" are frequently used to deport migrant women while their rapists and profiteers remain at large. At the same time, the carceral response overlooks the importance of exit options for survivors. Laws criminalizing marital rape or workplace assault won't help women with nowhere else to go, nor those with no way to get there. Under such conditions, no feminist with even a shred of sensitivity to class and race can endorse a carceral response to gender violence.

Equally inadequate are the "market-based solutions" proffered by femocrats. From their lofty perches at global financial institutions, these progressive neoliberals in skirts propose to shield their less fortunate Southern sisters from violence by lending them small sums of money to start their own businesses. The evidence that microloans actually reduce domestic violence or promote women's independence from men is spotty at best. However, one effect is crystal clear: *microlending increases women's dependence on their creditors*. By tightening the noose of debt around the necks of poor and working-class women, this approach to gender violence inflicts a violence of its own.

Feminism for the 99 percent rejects both carceral and femocratic approaches to gender violence. We know that gender violence under capitalism is not a disruption of the regular order of things, but a systemic condition. Deeply anchored in the social order, it can neither be understood nor redressed in isolation from the larger complex of capitalist violence: the biopolitical violence of laws that deny reproductive freedom; the economic violence of the market, the bank, the landlord, and the loan shark; the state violence of police, courts, and prison guards; the transnational violence of border agents, migration regimes, and imperial armies; the symbolic violence of mainstream culture that colonizes our minds, distorts our bodies, and silences our voices; and the "slow" environmental violence that eats away at our communities and habitats.

These dynamics, while endemic to capitalism, have sharply escalated during the present period of crisis. In the name of "individual responsibility," neoliberalism has slashed public funding for social provisions. In some cases, it has marketized public services, turning them into direct profit streams; in others, it has shunted them back to individual families, forcing them—and especially the women within them—to bear the entire burden of care. The effect is to further encourage gender violence.

In the United States, the crash of the mortgage market disproportionately hit women of color, who suffered the highest rates of eviction and were more likely to be forced to choose between homelessness and remaining in abusive relationships. In the UK, the powers that be responded to the financial collapse by further slashing public services—first and foremost, funding for domestic violence shelters. In the Caribbean, an increase in food and fuel prices coincided with cuts in public funding for social services, producing a rise in gender violence. These moves were accompanied by a proliferation of normalizing, disciplinary propaganda. Repeated admonitions to be a "good" wife or to have more children turn all too quickly into justifications for violence against those who fail to conform to normative gender roles and identities.

Today, moreover, anti-labor laws exacerbate violence in economic sectors that rely heavily on women workers. In export-processing zones (EPZs), such as the 3,000 maquiladoras in Mexico, gender violence is widely deployed as a tool of labor discipline. Bosses and managers in the factories use serial rape, verbal abuse, and humiliating body searches to increase productivity and discourage labor organizing. Once entrenched in EPZs, it is only a matter of time before these practices are generalized through the whole of society—including in working-class homes.

In capitalist societies, then, gender violence is not freestanding. On the contrary, it has deep roots within a social order that entwines women's subordination with the gendered organization of work and the dynamics of capital accumulation. Viewed this way, it is not surprising that the #MeToo movement began as a protest against workplace abuse, nor that the first statement of solidarity with the women in show business came from immigrant farmworkers in California: they immediately recognized Harvey Weinstein not simply as a predator, but as a powerful *boss*, able to dictate who would be allowed to work in Hollywood and who would not.

Violence, in all its forms, is integral to the everyday functioning of capitalist society—for it is only through a mix of brute coercion and constructed consent that the system can sustain itself in the best of times. One form of violence cannot be stopped without stopping the others. Vowing to eradicate them all, feminists for the 99 percent aim to connect the struggle against gender violence to the fight against all forms of violence in capitalist society—and against the social system that undergirds them.

Thesis 7: Capitalism tries to regulate sexuality. We want to liberate it.

At first sight, today's sexual struggles present an unambiguous choice. On one side stand the forces of sexual reaction; on the other, those of sexual liberalism. The reactionaries seek to outlaw sexual practices that they claim violate enduring family values or divine law. Determined to uphold those supposedly timeless principles, they would stone "adulterers," cane lesbians, or subject gay people to "conversion therapy." By contrast, the liberals fight for the legal rights of sexual dissidents and minorities. Endorsing state recognition of once-tabooed relationships and despised identities, they support "marriage equality" and LGBTQ+ access to the ranks of the military. Whereas the first side seeks to rehabilitate regressive archaisms—patriarchy, homophobia, sexual repression—the second stands for modernity—individual freedom, self-expression, and sexual diversity. How could the choice be anything but a no-brainer?

In reality, though, neither side is what it appears. On the one hand, the sexual authoritarianism we encounter today is anything but archaic. While presented as timeless divine commands or age-old customs, the prohibitions it aims to establish are in fact "neo-traditional": reactive responses to capitalist development, as modern as what they oppose. And by the same token, the sexual rights promised by liberal opponents are conceived in terms that presuppose capitalist forms of modernity; far from enabling real liberation, they are normalizing, statist, and consumerist.

To see why this is so, consider the genealogy of this opposition. Capitalist societies have always tried to regulate sexuality, but the means and methods have varied historically. In the system's early days, before capitalist relations had been pervasively established, it was left to preexisting authorities (especially churches and communities) to establish and enforce the norms that distinguished acceptable from sinful sex. Later, as capitalism proceeded to reshape the whole of society, it incubated new bourgeois norms and modes of regulation—including state-sanctioned gender binarism and heteronormativity. Confined neither to the capitalist metropole nor to the bourgeois classes, these "modern" norms of gender and sexuality were broadly diffused, including via colonialism and through mass culture; and they were widely enforced by repressive and administrative state power, including by family-based criteria of entitlement to social provisions. But they did not go unchallenged. On the contrary, these norms collided not only with older sexual regimes, but also with still-newer aspirations for sexual freedom, which found expression, especially in cities, in gay and lesbian subcultures and in avant-garde enclaves.

Later developments restructured that configuration. In the aftermath of the 1960s, the bourgeois current softened, while the liberationist strand overflowed the subcultures that originated it and went mainstream. As a result, dominant factions of both those streams are increasingly united in a new project: *to normalize once taboo forms of sex within an expanded zone of state regulation, and in a capital-friendly guise that encourages individualism, domesticity, and commodity consumption.*

What lies behind this new configuration is a decisive shift in the nature of capitalism. Increasingly financialized, globalized, and de-familialized, capital is no longer implacably opposed to queer and non-cis sex/gender formations. Nor do large corporations still insist on one and only one normative form of family or sex; many of them are now willing to permit significant numbers of their employees to live outside heterosexual families— that is, provided they toe the line, both at the workplace and at the mall. In the marketplace, too, sexual dissidence finds a niche as a source of enticing advertising images, product lines, lifestyle commodities, and prepackaged pleasures. Sex sells in capitalist society—and neoliberalism merchandizes it in many flavors.

Today's struggles over sexuality take the stage at a time of tremendous gender fluidity among the young, and amid burgeoning queer and feminist movements. It is also a time of significant legal victories, including formal gender equality, LGBTQ+ rights, and marriage equality—all now enshrined in law in a growing list of countries throughout the world. These victories are the fruits of hard-fought battles, even as they also reflect momentous social and cultural changes associated with neoliberalism. Nevertheless, they are inherently fragile and constantly threatened.

New legal rights do not stop the assault on LGBTQ+ people, who continue to experience gender and sexual violence, symbolic misrecognition, and social discrimination.

In fact, financialized capitalism is fueling a sexual backlash of major proportions. It is not "just" the "incels," who murder women to avenge the "theft" of female sexuality from its "rightful male owners." Not "just" the card-carrying reactionaries who propose to protect "their" women and families from cutthroat individualism, crass consumerism, and "vice." The reaction also includes fast-growing right-wing populist movements that gain mass support by identifying some *real* downsides of capitalist modernity—including its failure to protect families and communities from the ravages of the market. However, both neo-traditional and right-wing populist forces twist those legitimate grievances to fuel precisely the sort of opposition that capital can well afford. Theirs is a mode of "protection" that pins the rap on sexual freedom while obscuring the true source of danger, which is capital.

Sexual reaction finds its mirror image in sexual liberalism. The latter is tied, even in the best-case scenarios, to policies that deprive the overwhelming majority of the social and material prerequisites needed to realize their new formal freedoms—consider, for instance, how states that claim to recognize the rights of trans people simultaneously refuse to defray the costs of transition. Sexual liberalism is also tied to state-centered regulatory regimes that normalize and enforce the monogamous family, conformity to which is the price of acceptance for gays and lesbians. While appearing to valorize individual freedom, sexual liberalism leaves unchallenged the structural conditions that fuel homophobia and transphobia, including the role of the family in social reproduction.

Outside the family, too, what passes for sexual liberation often recycles capitalist values. New heterosexual cultures, based on hook-ups and online dating, urge young women to "own" their sexuality, but continue to rate them by their looks as defined by men. Exhorting "self-ownership," neoliberal discourses pressure girls to pleasure boys, licensing male sexual selfishness in exemplary capitalist fashion.

Likewise, new forms of "gay normality" presuppose *capitalist normality*. Emerging gay middle classes are defined in many countries by their mode of consumption and claim to respectability. Not only does this stratum's acceptance coexist with the continuing marginalization and repression of poor queer people, especially queer people of color; it also figures in "pinkwashing," as those in power cite their acceptance of "right-thinking, right-living" gays to legitimate imperialist and neocolonial projects. For example, Israeli state agencies cite their superior "gay-friendly" culture to justify their brutal subjugation of "backward, homophobic" Palestinians. Similarly, some European liberals invoke their own "enlightened toleration" of LGBTQ+ individuals in order to legitimate hostility toward Muslims, whom they equate indiscriminately with reaction, while giving non-Muslim sex-authoritarians a free pass.

The upshot is that today's liberation movements are caught between a rock and a hard place: one side wants to deliver women and LGBTQ+ people to religious or patriarchal domination, while the other would hand us over on a platter for direct predation by capital. Feminists for the 99 percent refuse to play this game. Rejecting both neoliberal co-optation and neo-traditional homophobia and misogyny, we want to revive the radical spirit of the 1969 Stonewall uprising in New York, of "sex-positive" currents of feminism from Alexandra Kollontai to Gayle Rubin, and of the historic lesbian and gay support campaign for the 1984 British miner's strike. We fight to liberate sexuality not only from procreation and normative family forms, but also from the restrictions of gender, class, and race, and from the deformations of statism and consumerism. We know, however, that to realize this dream we must build a new, noncapitalist form of society that assures the material bases of sexual liberation, among them generous public support for social reproduction, redesigned for a much wider range of families and personal associations.

Thesis 8: Capitalism was born from racist and colonial violence. Feminism for the 99 percent is anti-racist and anti-imperialist.

Today, as in previous moments of acute capitalist crisis, "race" has become a red-hot issue, inflamed and intensely contested. Encouraged by demagogues purporting to champion aggrieved majorities, an aggressively ethnonationalist right-wing populism dispenses with "mere" dog whistles in favor of full-throated blasts of European and white supremacy. Craven centrist governments join their outright-racist counterparts in blocking the entry of migrants and refugees, seizing their children and separating their families, interning them in camps, or leaving them to drown at sea. Meanwhile, police in Brazil, the United States, and elsewhere continue to murder people of color with impunity, while courts cage them in for-profit prisons in record numbers and for extended terms.

Many are scandalized by these developments, and some have tried to fight back. Activists in Germany,

Brazil, the United States, and elsewhere have turned out in force to protest racist police violence and demonstrations by white supremacists. Some are struggling to give new meaning to the term "abolition," demanding an end to incarceration and the elimination of ICE, the US government agency charged with enforcing immigration restrictions. Nevertheless, many anti-racist forces limit their interventions to moral denunciation. Others choose to play with fire–witness those currents of left-wing parties in Europe that propose to "co-opt" the Right by themselves opposing immigration.

In this situation, feminists, like everyone else, must take sides. Historically, however, the feminist record in dealing with race has been mixed, at best. Influential white US suffragists indulged in explicitly racist rants after the Civil War, when black men were granted the vote and they were not. In the same period, and well into the twentieth century, leading British feminists defended colonial rule in India on racially coded "civilizational" grounds, as necessary to "raise up brown women from their lowly condition." Even today, prominent feminists in European countries justify anti-Muslim policies in similar terms.

Feminism's historic entanglement with racism has also assumed "subtler" forms. Even where they were not explicitly or intentionally racist, liberal and radical feminists alike have defined "sexism" and "gender issues" in ways that falsely universalize the situation of white, middle-class women. Abstracting gender from race (and class), they have prioritized "women's" need to escape from domesticity and "go out to work"—as if all of us were suburban housewives! Following the same logic, leading white feminists in the United States have insisted that black women could only be truly feminist if they prioritized an imagined post- or non-racial sisterhood over anti-racist solidarity with black men. It is only thanks to decades of determined pushback by feminists of color that such views are increasingly seen for what they are and are now rejected by growing numbers of feminists of every hue.

Feminists for the 99 percent forthrightly acknowledge this shameful history and resolve to break decisively with it. We understand that *nothing that deserves the name of "women's liberation" can be achieved in a racist, imperialist society*. But we also understand that the root of the problem is capitalism, and that racism and imperialism are integral to the latter. This social system, which prides itself on "free labor" and "the wage contract," could only get started thanks to violent colonial plunder, the "commercial hunting of black-skins" in Africa, their forcible conscription into "New World" slavery, and the dispossession of indigenous peoples.

But far from ceasing once capitalism got off the ground, the racialized expropriation of unfree or dependent peoples has served ever since as a hidden enabling condition for the profitable exploitation of "free labor." The distinction between free exploited "workers" and dependent expropriated "others" has assumed different forms throughout capitalism's history—in slavery, colonialism, apartheid, and the international division of labor—and it has blurred at times. But in every phase, it has coincided, however roughly, with the global color line. In every phase, too, up to and including the present, the expropriation of racialized people has enabled capital to increase its profits by confiscating natural resources and human capacities for whose replenishment and reproduction it does not pay. For systemic reasons, capitalism has always created classes of racialized human beings, whose persons and work are devalued and subject to expropriation. *A feminism that is truly anti-racist and anti-imperialist must also be anticapitalist.*

That proposition is as true as ever now, when racialized expropriation is proceeding on steroids. Intensifying dispossession by debt, today's neoliberal capitalism promotes racial oppression throughout the world. In the "postcolonial" global South, debt-fueled corporate land grabs drive masses of indigenous and tribal peoples from their lands—and in some cases to suicide. At the same time, the "restructuring" of sovereign debt sends the ratio of interest to GDP through the roof, forcing supposedly independent states to slash social spending, and condemning future generations of Southern workers to devote an ever-growing share of their labor to the repayment of global lenders. In these ways, racialized expropriation continues alongside, and is intertwined with, a rise in exploitation propelled by the relocation of much manufacturing to the global South.

In the global North, too, this oppression continues apace. As low-waged, precarious service work replaces unionized industrial labor, wages fall below the bare minimum necessary to live a decent life, especially in jobs where racialized workers predominate. Not only are these workers forced to take on multiple jobs and to borrow against future wages in order to survive; they are also targeted for hyper-expropriative payday and subprime loans. The social wage is declining as well, as services that used to be provided publicly are offloaded onto families and communities—which is to say, chiefly onto minority and immigrant women. Likewise, tax revenues previously dedicated to public infrastructure are diverted to debt service, with especially disastrous effects for communities of color—spatially segregated and long deprived of public funds for schools and hospitals, housing and transport, provision of clean air and water. At every level and in every region, financialized capitalism brings major new waves of racialized expropriation.

The effects of this global pyramid scheme are gendered as well. Today, millions of black and migrant women are employed as caregivers and domestic workers. Often undocumented and far from their families, they are simultaneously exploited and expropriated—forced to work precariously and on the cheap, deprived of rights, and subject to abuses of every stripe. Forged by global care chains, their oppression enables better conditions for more privileged women, who avoid (some) domestic work and pursue demanding professions. How ironic, then, that some of these privileged women invoke women's rights in support of political campaigns to jail black men as rapists, to persecute migrants and Muslims, and to require that black and Muslim women assimilate to dominant culture!

The truth is that racism, imperialism, and ethno-nationalism are essential buttresses of *generalized* misogyny and the control over *all* women's bodies. Because their operation harms *all* of us, all of us need to fight them tooth and nail. But abstract proclamations of global sisterhood are counterproductive. Treating what is really the goal of a political process as if it were given at the outset, they convey a false impression of homogeneity. The reality is that, although we all suffer misogynist oppression in capitalist society, our oppression assumes different forms. Not always immediately visible, the links between those forms of oppression must be revealed politically—that is, through conscious efforts to build solidarity. Only in this way, by struggling in and through our diversity, can we achieve the combined power we need if we hope to transform society.

Thesis 9: Fighting to reverse capital's destruction of the earth, feminism for the 99 percent is eco-socialist.

Today's crisis of capitalism is also an ecological crisis. Capitalism has always sought to bolster its profits by commandeering natural resources, which it treats as free and infinite, and which it often steals outright. Structurally primed to appropriate nature without any regard for replenishment, capitalism periodically destabilizes its own ecological conditions of possibility—whether by exhausting the soil and depleting mineral wealth, or by poisoning the water and air.

While today's ecological crisis is not the first in capitalism's history, it is surely the most global and pressing yet. The climate change now threatening the planet is a direct outgrowth of capital's historic resort to fossilized energy in order to power its signature mass-production industrial factories. It was not "humanity" in general but *capital* that extracted carbonized deposits formed over hundreds of millions of years beneath the crust of the earth; and it was *capital* that consumed them in the blink of an eye with total disregard for replenishment or the impacts of pollution and greenhouse gas emissions. Subsequent shifts, first from coal to oil, and then to fracking and natural gas, have only ramped up carbon emissions, while disproportionately offloading the "externalities" onto poor communities, often communities of color, in the global North and the global South.

If today's ecological crisis is directly tied to capitalism, it also reproduces and worsens women's oppression. Women occupy the front lines of the present ecological crisis, making up 80 percent of climate refugees. In the global South, they consti-tute the vast majority of the rural workforce, even as they also bear responsibility for the lion's share of social-reproductive labor. Because of their key role in providing food, clothing, and shelter for their families, women play an outsized part in coping with drought, pollution, and the overexploitation of land. Likewise, poor women of color in the global North are disproportionately vulnerable. Subject to environmental racism, they constitute the backbone of communities subject to flooding and lead poisoning.

Women are also at the forefront of struggles against the growing ecological catastrophe. Decades ago in the United States, the militant leftwing group Women Strike for Peace agitated against atomic weapons that had deposited Strontium-90 in our bones. Today, women spearhead the Water Protectors' fight against the Dakota Access Pipeline in the United States. In Peru, they powered Máxima Acuña's successful battle against the US mining giant Newmont. In North India, Garhwali women are fighting against the construction of three hydro-electric dams. Across the globe women lead myriad struggles against the privatization of water and seed, and for the preservation of biodiversity and sustainable farming.

In all these cases, women model new, integrated forms of struggle that challenge the tendency of mainstream environmentalists to frame the defense of "nature" and the material well-being of human communities as mutually antithetical. In their refusal to separate ecological issues from those of social reproduction, these women-led movements represent a powerful anti-corporate and anti-capitalist alternative to "green capitalist" projects that do nothing to stop global warming while enriching those who speculate in "emissions permits," "ecosystem services," "carbon offsets," and "environmental derivatives." Unlike those "green finance" projects, which dissolve nature into a miasma of quantitative abstraction, women's struggles focus on the real world, in which social justice, the well-being of human communities, and the sustainability of nonhuman nature are inextricably bound up together.

The liberation of women and the preservation of our planet from ecological disaster go hand in hand—with each other and with the overcoming of capitalism.

Thesis 10: Capitalism is incompatible with real democracy and peace. Our answer is feminist internationalism.

Today's crisis is also political. Paralyzed by gridlock and hobbled by global finance, states that once claimed to be democratic routinely fail to address pressing problems at all, let alone in the public interest; most of them punt on climate change and financial reform, when they don't openly block the path to solutions. Captured by corporate power and enfeebled by debt, governments are increasingly seen by their subjects as handmaidens of capital, which dance to the tune of central banks and international investors, IT mammoths, energy magnates, and war profiteers. Is it any wonder that masses of people throughout the world have given up on mainstream parties and politicians that have promoted neoliberalism, including those of the center-left?

Political crisis is rooted in the institutional structure of capitalist society. This system divides "the political" from "the economic," the "legitimate violence" of the state from the "silent compulsion" of the market. The effect is to declare vast swaths of social life off limits to democratic control and turn them over to direct corporate domination. By virtue of its very structure, therefore, capitalism deprives us of the ability to decide collectively exactly what and how much to produce, on what energic basis, and through what kinds of social relations. It robs us, too, of the capacity to determine how we want to use the social surplus we collectively produce, how we want to relate to nature and to future generations, and how we want to organize the work of social reproduction and its relation to that of production. Capitalism, in sum, is fundamentally antidemocratic.

At the same time, capitalism necessarily generates an imperialist world geography. This system authorizes powerful states of the global North to prey on weaker ones: to siphon value from them through trade regimes tilted against them and to crush them with debt; to threaten them with military intervention and the withholding of "aid." The effect is to deny political protection to much of the world's population. Apparently, the democratic aspirations of billions of people in the global South are not even worth coopting. They can simply be ignored or brutally repressed.

Everywhere, too, capital tries to have it both ways. On the one hand, it freeloads off of public power, availing itself of legal regimes that secure private property and the repressive forces that suppress opposition, helping itself to infrastructures necessary for accumulation and the regulatory agencies tasked with managing crises. On the other hand, the thirst for profit periodically tempts some factions of the capitalist class to rebel against public power, which they badmouth as inferior to markets and scheme to weaken. When such short-term interests trump long-term survival, capital assumes the form of a tiger that eats its own tail. It threatens to destroy the very political institutions that it depends upon for survival.

Capitalism's tendency to generate political crisis—at work even in the best of times—has reached a fever pitch. The current neoliberal regime openly wields not only military hardware, but also the weapon of debt, as it brazenly targets any public powers and political forces that might challenge it—for example, by nullifying elections and referenda that reject austerity, as in Greece in 2015, and by preventing those that might do so, as in Brazil in 2017–18. Throughout the world, leading capitalist interests (Big Fruit, Big Pharma, Big Oil, and Big Arms) have systematically promoted authoritarianism and repression, coups d'états and imperial wars. In direct refutation of the claims of its partisans, this social system reveals itself to be structurally incompatible with democracy.

It is once again women who are major casualties of capitalism's current political crisis—and they are also principal actors in the struggle for an emancipatory resolution. For us, however, the solution is not simply to install more women in the citadels of power. Having long been excluded from the public sphere, we have had to fight tooth and nail to be heard on matters—such as sexual assault and harassment—that have been routinely dismissed as "private." Ironically, however, our claims are often ventriloquized by elite "progressives" who inflect them in terms favorable to capital: they invite us to identify with and vote for women politicians, however unsavory, who ask us to celebrate *their* ascent to positions of power—as if it struck a blow for *our* liberation. But there is nothing feminist about ruling-class women who do the dirty work of bombing other countries and sustaining regimes of apartheid; of backing neocolonial interventions in the name of humanitarianism, while remaining silent about the genocides perpetrated by their own governments; of expropriating defenseless populations through structural adjustment, imposed debt, and forced austerity.

In reality, women are the first victims of colonial occupation and war throughout the world. They face systematic harassment, political rape, and enslavement, while enduring the murder and maiming of their loved ones, and the destruction of the infrastructures that enabled them to provide for themselves and their families in the first place. We stand in solidarity with *these* women—not with warmongers in skirts, who demand gender and sexual liberation for their kin alone. To the state bureaucrats and financial managers, both male and female, who purport to justify their warmongering by claiming to liberate brown and black women, we say: *Not in our name.*

Thesis 11: Feminism for the 99 percent calls on all radical movements to join together in a common anticapitalist insurgency.

Feminists for the 99 percent do not operate in isolation from other movements of resistance and rebellion. We do not separate ourselves from battles against climate change or exploitation in the workplace; nor do we stand aloof from struggles against institutional racism and dispossession. Those struggles are *our* struggles, part and parcel of the struggle to dismantle capitalism, without which there can be no end to gender and sexual oppression. The upshot is clear: feminism for the 99 percent must join forces with other anticapitalist movements across the globe—with environmentalist, antiracist, anti-imperialist, and LGBTQ+ movements and labor unions. *We must ally, above all, with left-wing, anticapitalist currents of those movements that also champion the 99 percent.*

This path pits us squarely against both of the principal political options that capital now offers. We reject not only reactionary populism but also progressive neoliberalism. In fact, it is by splitting both those alliances that we intend to build our movement. In the case of progressive-neoliberalism, we aim to separate the mass of working-class women, immigrants, and people of color from the lean-in feminists, the meritocratic anti-racists and anti-homophobes, and the corporate-diversity and green-capitalism shills who hijacked their concerns and inflected them in capital-friendly terms. With respect to reactionary populism, we aim to separate working-class communities from the forces promoting militarism, xenophobia, and ethno-nationalism that falsely present themselves as defenders of the "common man," while promoting plutocracy on the sly. Our strategy is to win over the working-class fractions of both of those pro-capitalist political blocs. In this way, we seek to build an anti-capitalist force that is large and powerful enough to transform society.

Struggle is both an opportunity and a school. It can transform those who participate in it, challenging our prior understandings of ourselves and reshaping our views of the world. Struggle can deepen our comprehension of our own oppression—what causes it, who benefits, and what must be done to overcome it. And further, it can prompt us to reinterpret our interests, reframe our hopes, and expand our sense of what is possible. Finally, the experience of struggle can also induce us to rethink who should count as an ally and who as an enemy. It can broaden the circle of solidarity among the oppressed and sharpen our antagonism to our oppressors.

The operative word here is "can." Everything depends on our ability to develop a guiding perspective that neither simply celebrates nor brutally obliterates the differences among us. Contra fashionable ideologies of "multiplicity," the various oppressions we suffer do not form an inchoate, contingent plurality. Although each has its own distinctive forms and characteristics, all are rooted in, and reinforced by, one and the same social system. It is by naming that system as *capitalism*, and by joining together to fight against it, that we can best overcome the divisions among us that capital cultivates—divisions of culture, race, ethnicity, ability, sexuality, and gender.

But we must understand capitalism in the right way. Contra narrow, old-school understandings, industrial wage labor is not the sum total of the working class; nor is its exploitation the apex of capitalist domination. To insist on its primacy is not to foster, but rather to weaken, class solidarity. In reality, class solidarity is best advanced by reciprocal recognition of the relevant differences among us— our disparate structural situations, experiences, and sufferings; our specific needs, desires, and demands; and the varied organizational forms through which we can best achieve them. In this way, feminism for the 99 percent seeks to overcome familiar, stale oppositions between "identity politics" and "class politics."

Rejecting the zero-sum framework capitalism constructs for us, feminism for the 99 percent aims to unite existing and future movements into a broad-based global insurgency. Armed with a vision that is at once feminist, anti-racist, and anticapitalist, we pledge to play a major role in shaping our future.

Postface

Beginning in the middle

Writing a feminist manifesto is a daunting task. Anyone who tries it today stands on the shoulders—and in the shadow—of Marx and Engels. Their 1848 *Communist Manifesto* began with a memorable line: "A spectre is haunting Europe." The "spectre," of course, was communism, a revolutionary project they depicted as the culmination of working-class struggles, viewed as on the march: unifying, internationalizing, and metamorphosing into a world-historical force that would eventually abolish capitalism—and with it, all exploitation, domination, and alienation.

We found this predecessor immensely inspiring, not least because it rightly identifies capitalism as the ultimate basis of oppression in modern society.

But it complicated our task, not only because *The Communist Manifesto* is a literary masterpiece—hence, a tough act to follow—but also because 2018 is not 1848. It is true that we, too, live in a world of tremendous social and political upheaval—which we, too, understand as a crisis of capitalism. But today's world is much more globalized than that of Marx and Engels, and the upheavals traversing it are by no means confined to Europe. Likewise, we, too, encounter conflicts over nation, race/ethnicity, and religion, in addition to those of class. But our world also encompasses politicized fault lines unknown to them: sexuality, disability, and ecology; and its gender struggles have a breadth and intensity that Marx and Engels could scarcely have imagined. Faced as we are with a more fractured and heterogeneous political landscape, it is not so easy for us to imagine a globally unified revolutionary force.

As latecomers, moreover, we are also more aware than Marx and Engels could possibly have been of the many ways in which emancipatory movements can go wrong. The historical memory we inherit includes the degeneration of the Bolshevik Revolution into the absolutist Stalinist state, European social democracy's capitulation to nationalism and war, and a slew of authoritarian regimes installed in the aftermath of anti-colonial struggles throughout the global South. Especially important for us is the recuperation of the emancipatory movements of our own time, which have become allies of, and alibis for, the forces that fostered neoliberalism. This latter experience has been painful for left-wing feminists, as we have witnessed mainstream liberal currents of our movement reduce our cause to the meritocratic advancement of the few.

This history could not fail to shape our expectations differently than those of Marx and Engels. Whereas they were writing in an era where capitalism was still relatively young, we face a wily, aging system, far more adept at co-optation and coercion. And today's political landscape is replete with traps. As we explained in our *Manifesto*, the most dangerous trap for feminists lies in thinking that our current political options are limited to two: on the one hand, a "progressive" variant of neoliberalism, which diffuses an elitist, corporate version of feminism to cast an emancipatory veneer over a predatory, oligarchic agenda; on the other, a reactionary variant of neoliberalism, which pursues a similar, plutocratic agenda by other means—deploying misogynist and racist tropes to burnish its "populist" credentials. Certainly, these two forces are not identical. But both are mortal enemies of a genuinely emancipatory and majoritarian feminism.

Plus, they are mutually enabling: progressive neoliberalism created the conditions for the rise of reactionary populism and is now positioning itself as the go-to alternative to it.

Our *Manifesto* embodies a refusal to choose sides in this battle. Rejecting a menu that limits our choices to two different strategies for managing capitalist crisis, we wrote it to forward an alternative to both. Committed not simply to managing but to *resolving* the present crisis, we sought to make visible, and practicable, some latent emancipatory possibilities that the current alignments obscure. Determined to break up liberal feminism's cozy alliance with finance capital, we proposed another feminism, a *feminism for the 99 percent*.

We came to this project after having worked together on the 2017 women's strike in the United States. Prior to that, each of us had written individually about the relation between capitalism and gender oppression. Cinzia Arruzza had parsed the fraught relations between feminism and socialism, both historically and theoretically. Tithi Bhattacharya had theorized the implications of social reproduction for the concepts of class and class struggle. Nancy Fraser had developed enlarged conceptions of capitalism and capitalist crisis, of which the crisis of social reproduction forms one strand.

Notwithstanding these different emphases, we joined forces to write this *Manifesto* because of a shared understanding of the present conjuncture. For all three of us, this moment represents a crucial juncture in the history of feminism and capitalism, a juncture that demands, and enables, an intervention. In this context, our decision to write a feminist manifesto was tied to a political objective: we sought to effect a rescue operation and course correction—to reorient feminist struggles in a time of political confusion.

Reconceptualizing capitalism and its crisis

The conjuncture our *Manifesto* responds to is best understood as a *crisis*. But we don't intend that word in the loose and obvious sense that things are bad. Although present calamities and sufferings are horrific, what justifies our use of the term "crisis" is something more: the numerous harms we experience today are neither mutually unrelated nor the products of chance. They stem, instead, from the societal system that underlies all of them—a system that generates them not accidentally but as a matter of course, by virtue of its constitutive dynamics.

Our *Manifesto* names that social system *capitalism* and characterizes the present crisis as a crisis *of capitalism*. But we do not understand those terms in the usual way. As feminists, we appreciate that capitalism is not just an economic system, but something larger: an institutionalized social order that also encompasses the apparently "noneconomic" relations and practices that sustain the official economy. Behind capitalism's official institutions—wage labor, production, exchange, and finance—stand their necessary supports and enabling conditions: families, communities, nature; territorial states, political organizations, and civil societies; and not least of all, massive amounts and multiple forms of unwaged and expropriated labor, including much of the work of social reproduction, still performed largely by women and often uncompensated. These, too, are constitutive elements of capitalist society—and sites of struggle within it.

From this expansive understanding of capitalism follows our *Manifesto*'s broad view of capitalist crisis. Without denying its inherent tendency to spawn intermittent market crashes, bankruptcy chains, and mass unemployment, we recognize that capitalism also harbors other, "noneconomic," contradictions and crisis tendencies. It contains, for example, an *ecological contradiction*: an inherent tendency to reduce nature to a "tap" dispensing energy and raw materials on one hand, and to a "sink" for absorbing waste on the other—both capacities that capital appropriates freely but does not replenish. As a result, capitalist societies are structurally inclined to destabilize the habitats that sustain communities and to destroy the ecosystems that sustain life.

Likewise, this social formation houses a *political contradiction*: a built-in tendency to limit the purview of politics, devolving fundamental matters of life and death to the rule of "the markets," and turning state institutions that are supposed to serve the public into capital's servants. For systemic reasons, therefore, capitalism is disposed to frustrate democratic aspirations, to hollow out rights and defang public powers, and to generate brutal repression, endless wars, and crises of governance.

Finally, capitalist society harbors a *social-reproductive contradiction*: a tendency to commandeer for capital's benefit as much "free" reproductive labor as possible, without any concern for its replenishment. As a result, it periodically gives rise to "crises of care," which exhaust women, ravage families, and stretch social energies to the breaking point.

In our *Manifesto*, in other words, capitalist crisis is not only economic but also ecological, political, and social-reproductive. In every case, moreover, the root is the same: capital's inherent drive to free-ride on its own indispensable background conditions—prerequisites for whose reproduction it aims not to pay. Those conditions include the atmosphere's ability to absorb carbon emissions; the state's capacity to defend property, put down rebellion, and safeguard money; and, of central importance for us, the unwaged work of forming and sustaining human beings. Without them, capital could neither exploit "workers" nor succeed in accumulating profits. But if it can't live without these background conditions, its logic also drives it to disavow them. If forced to pay the full replacement costs of nature, public power, and social reproduction, capital's profits would dwindle to the vanishing point. Better to cannibalize the system's own conditions of possibility than to jeopardize accumulation!

It is therefore a premise of our *Manifesto* that capitalism harbors multiple contradictions, above and beyond those that stem from its official economy. In "normal" times, the system's crisis tendencies remain more or less latent, afflicting "only" those populations deemed disposable and powerless. But these are not normal times. Today, *all* of capitalism's contradictions have reached the boiling point. Virtually no one—with the partial exception of the 1 percent—escapes the impacts of political dislocation, economic precarity and social-reproductive depletion. And climate change, of course, threatens to destroy all life on the planet. The recognition is growing, too, that these catastrophic developments are so deeply intertwined that none can be resolved apart from the others.

What is social reproduction?

Our *Manifesto* deals with every facet of the present crisis. But we take a special interest in the social-reproductive aspect, which is structurally connected to gender asymmetry. So, let us enquire more deeply: what exactly *is* social reproduction?

Consider the case of "Luo." A Taiwanese mother identified only by her last name, she filed a suit in 2017 against her son, claiming recompense for the time and money she had invested in his upbringing. Luo had raised two sons as a single mother, putting both of them through dental school. In return, she expected them to take care of her in her old age. When one of the sons failed to satisfy her expectations, she sued him. In an unprecedented ruling, the Taiwanese Supreme Court ordered the son to pay his mother US$967,000 as his "upbringing" cost.

Luo's case illustrates three fundamental features of life under capitalism. First, it discloses a human universal that capitalism would prefer to ignore and tries to hide: that enormous amounts of time and resources are necessary to birth, care for, and maintain human beings. Second, it underlines that much of the work of creating and/or maintaining human beings is still done by women in our society. Finally, it reveals that in the normal course of things, capitalist society accords no value to this work, even while depending upon it.

Luo's case also prompts us to entertain a fourth proposition, which figures centrally in our *Manifesto*: that capitalist society is composed of two inextricably braided but mutually opposed imperatives—the need of the system to sustain itself through its signature process of *profit-making*, versus the need of human beings to sustain themselves through processes that we called *people-making*. "Social reproduction" refers to the second imperative. It encompasses activities that sustain human beings as *embodied social beings* who must not only eat and sleep but also raise their children, care for their families, and maintain their communities, all while pursuing their hopes for the future.

These people-making activities occur in one form or another in every society. In *capitalist* societies, however, they must also serve another master— namely, capital, which requires that social-reproductive work produce and replenish "labor power." Bent on securing an adequate supply of that "peculiar commodity" at the lowest possible cost to itself, capital offloads the work of social reproduction onto women, communities, and states, all the while twisting it into forms best suited to maximize its profits. Various branches of feminist theory, including Marxist feminism, socialist feminism, and social reproduction theory, have analyzed the contradictions between the profit-making and people-making tendencies in capitalist societies, exposing capital's inherent drive to instrumentalize the second to the needs of the first.

Readers of Marx's *Capital* know about exploitation: the injustice that capital inflicts on waged workers at the point of production. In that setting, workers are supposed to be paid enough to cover their living expenses, while in reality they produce more. In a nutshell, our bosses require us to work more hours than necessary to reproduce ourselves, our families, and the infrastructures of our societies. They appropriate the surplus we produce in the form of profit on behalf of the owners and shareholders.

Social reproduction theorists do not so much reject this picture as note its incompleteness. Like Marxist and socialist feminists, we raise some pesky questions: What did the worker have to do *before* she arrived at work? Who cooked her dinner, made her bed, and soothed her distress so that she could return to the job one tiring day after another? Did someone else do all this people-making work, or was it she herself who performed it—not only for herself but also for the other members of her family?

These questions disclose a truth that capitalism conspires to obscure: the waged work of profit-making could not exist without the (mostly) unwaged work of people-making. Thus, the capitalist institution of wage labor conceals something more than surplus value. It also conceals its birthmarks—the labor of social reproduction that is its condition of possibility. The social processes and institutions necessary for both kinds of "production"—that of people and that of profits—while analytically distinct, are nevertheless mutually constitutive.

The distinction between them, moreover, is itself an artifact of capitalist society. As we said, people-making work has always existed, and it has always been associated with women. But earlier societies knew no sharp division between "economic production" and social reproduction. Only with the advent of capitalism were those two aspects of social existence split apart. Production moved into factories, mines, and offices, where it was considered "economic" and remunerated with cash wages. Reproduction was relegated to "the family," where it was feminized and sentimentalized, defined as "care" as opposed to "work," performed for the sake of "love" as opposed to money. Or so we were told. In fact, capitalist societies have never located social reproduction exclusively in private households, but have always situated some of it in neighborhoods, grassroots communities, public institutions, and civil society; and they have long commodified *some* reproductive labor—although nowhere near as much as today.

Nevertheless, the division between profit-making and people-making points to a deep-seated tension at the heart of capitalist society. While capital strives systemically to increase profits, working-class people strive, conversely, to lead decent and meaningful lives as social beings. These are fundamentally irreconcilable goals, for capital's share of accumulation can only increase at the expense of our share in the life of society. Social practices that nourish our lives at home, and social services that nurture our lives outside of it, constantly threaten to cut into profits. Thus, a financial drive to reduce those costs and an ideological drive to undermine such labors are endemic to the system as a whole.

If capitalism's story was simply one in which profit-making vanquishes people-making, then the system could legitimately declare victory. But the history of capitalism is also shaped by struggles for decent and meaningful lives. It is no coincidence that wage struggles are often referred to as struggles over "bread and butter" issues. It is a mistake, however, to restrict those issues to workplace demands alone, as traditional labor movements have often done. They overlook the stormy, unsettled relationship between wages and life in a system where capital ordains the former as the only means to the latter. Working people do not struggle for the wage; rather, they struggle for the wage *because* they want bread and butter. The desire for sustenance is the determinant, not the consequence. Thus, struggles over food, housing, water, health care, or education are not always expressed through the mediated form of the wage—that is to say, as demands for higher wages within the workplace. Recall, for instance, that the two greatest revolutions of the modern era, the French and the Russian, began with bread riots led by women.

The true aim of social reproduction struggles is to establish the primacy of people-making over profit-making. They are never about bread alone. For this reason, a feminism for the 99 percent incarnates and fosters the *struggle for bread and roses*.

Crisis of social reproduction

In the conjuncture our *Manifesto* analyzes, social reproduction is the site of a major crisis. The basic reason, we argued, is that capitalism's treatment of social reproduction is contradictory. On the one hand, the system cannot function without this activity; on the other, it disavows the latter's costs and accords it little or no economic value. What this means is that the capacities available for social reproductive work are taken for granted, treated as free and infinitely available "gifts" that require no attention or replenishment. When the matter is considered at all, it is assumed that there will always be sufficient energies to produce the laborers and sustain the social connections on which economic production, and society more generally, depend. In fact, social-reproductive capacities are not infinite, and they can be stretched to the breaking point. When a society simultaneously withdraws public support for social reproduction and conscripts its chief providers into long and grueling hours of low-paid work, it depletes the very social capacities on which it relies.

This is exactly our situation today. The current, neoliberal form of capitalism is systematically depleting our collective and individual capacities to regenerate human beings and to sustain social bonds. At first sight this regime appears to be breaking down capitalism's constitutive gender division between productive and reproductive labor. Proclaiming the new ideal of the "two-earner family," neoliberalism recruits women massively into wage labor across the globe. But this ideal is a fraud; and the labor regime it is supposed to legitimate is anything but liberatory for women. What is presented as emancipation is in fact a system of intensified exploitation and expropriation. At the same time, it is also an engine of acute social-reproductive crisis.

It is true, of course, that a thin stratum of women derives some gains from neoliberalism as they enter prestigious professions and the lower rungs of corporate management, albeit on terms less favorable than those available to the men of their class. What awaits the vast majority, however, is something else: low-paid, precarious work—in sweatshops, export-processing zones, megacities' construction industries, corporatized agriculture, and the service sector—where poor, racialized, and immigrant women serve fast food and sell cheap stuff at megastores; clean offices, hotel rooms, and private homes; empty bedpans in hospitals and nursing homes; and care for the families of more privileged strata—often at the expense of, and sometimes far away from, their own.

Some of this work commodifies reproductive labor that was previously performed without pay. But if the effect of such commodification is to muddy capitalism's historical division between production and reproduction, it is equally certain that this outcome does *not* emancipate women. On the contrary, nearly all of us are still required to work "the second shift," even as more of our time and energy are appropriated by capital. And of course, the bulk of women's waged work is decidedly *un*-liberating. Precarious and poorly paid, and providing access neither to labor rights nor to social entitlements, it also fails to afford autonomy, self-realization, or the opportunity to acquire and exercise skills. What this work *does* provide, by contrast, is vulnerability to abuse and harassment.

Equally importantly, the wages we earn within this regime are often insufficient to cover the costs of our own social reproduction, let alone that of our families. Access to the wage of another household member helps, of course, but is still rarely enough. As a result, many of us are forced to work multiple "McJobs," traveling long distances between them via expensive, deteriorating, and unsafe means of transport. In comparison with the postwar era, the number of hours of waged work per household has skyrocketed, cutting deep into the time available to replenish ourselves, care for our families and friends, and maintain our homes and communities.

Far from inaugurating a feminist utopia, then, neo-liberal capitalism in reality generalizes exploitation.

Not just men, but women, too, are now forced to sell their labor power piecemeal—and cheaply—in order to survive. And that is not all: today's exploitation is overlaid with expropriation. Refusing to pay the costs of reproducing its own (increasingly feminized) labor force, capital is no longer content to appropriate "only" the surplus value its workers produce over and above their own means of subsistence. In addition, it now drills deep into the bodies, minds, and families of those it exploits, extracting not only surplus energies but also those needed for replenishment. Mining social reproduction as a further source of profit, it cuts into bone.

Capital's assault on social reproduction also proceeds through the retrenchment of public social services. In the previous social-democratic (or state-managed) phase of capitalist development, working classes in wealthy countries won some concessions from capital in the form of state support for social reproduction: pensions, unemployment insurance, child allowances, free public education, and health insurance. The result, however, was no golden age; the gains achieved by majority-ethnicity workers in the capitalist core rested on the often counterfactual assumption of women's dependency through the family wage, racial/ethnic exclusions from social security, heteronormative eligibility criteria for social welfare, and ongoing imperial expropriation in the "Third World." Nevertheless, these concessions offered partial protection for some from capital's inherent tendency to cannibalize social reproduction.

Neoliberal, financialized capitalism is a different animal altogether. Far from empowering states to stabilize social reproduction through public provision, it authorizes finance capital to discipline states and publics in the immediate interests of private investors. Its weapon of choice is debt. Finance capital lives off of *sovereign debt*, which it uses to outlaw even the mildest forms of social-democratic provision, coercing states to liberalize their economies, open their markets, and impose "austerity" on defenseless populations. Simultaneously, it proliferates *consumer debt*—from subprime mortgages to credit cards and student loans, from payday loans to microcredit—which it uses to discipline peasants and workers, to keep them subservient on the land and on the job, and to ensure that they continue to buy GMO seeds and cheap consumer goods at levels well above what their low wages would otherwise allow. In both ways, the regime sharpens capitalism's inherent contradiction between the imperative of accumulation and the requirements of social reproduction. Simultaneously demanding increased working hours and retrenched public services, it externalizes carework onto families and communities while diminishing their capacity to perform it.

The result is a mad scramble, on the part of women especially, to shoehorn social-reproductive responsibilities into the interstices of lives that capital demands be devoted primarily to its accumulation. Typically, this means off-loading carework onto less privileged others. The result is to forge "global care chains," as those who possess the means to do so hire poorer women, often migrants and/or members of racialized groups, to clean their homes or care for their children and aging parents, while they themselves pursue more lucrative work. But of course, that leaves the low-paid careworker scrambling to meet her own domestic and familial responsibilities, often by transferring them to other, still-poorer women, who in turn must do the same— and on and on, often across great distances.

This scenario fits the gendered strategies of indebted postcolonial states that have been subjected to "structural adjustment." Desperate for hard currency, some of these states have actively promoted women's emigration to perform paid carework abroad for the sake of remittances, while others have courted foreign direct investment by creating export-processing zones, often in industries (such as textiles and electronics assembly) that prefer to employ low-paid women workers, who are then subject to rampant labor and sexual violence. In both cases, social-reproductive capacities are further squeezed. Far from filling the care gap, the net effect is to displace it: from richer to poorer families, from the global North to the global South. The overall result is a new, *dualized* organization of social reproduction, commodified for those who can pay for it and privatized for those who cannot, as some in the second category provide carework in return for (low) wages for those in the first.

All of this adds up to what some call a "crisis of care." But that expression can easily mislead, for, as we argued in our *Manifesto*, this crisis is *structural*— part and parcel of the broader general crisis of contemporary capitalism. Given the latter's severity, it is no wonder that struggles over social reproduction have exploded over recent years. Northern feminists often describe their focus as the "balance between family and work." But struggles over social reproduction encompass much more—including grassroots community movements for housing, health care, food security, and an unconditional basic income; struggles for the rights of migrants, domestic workers, and public employees; campaigns to unionize social service workers in for-profit nursing homes, hospitals, and childcare centers; and struggles for public services such as day care and elder care, a shorter work week, and generous paid maternity and parental leave. Taken together, these claims are tantamount to a demand for a massive reorganization of the relation between production and reproduction: for social arrange-ments that prioritize people's lives and social connections over production for profit; for a world in which people of every gender, nationality, sexuality, and color combine social-reproductive activities with safe, well-remunerated, and harassment-free work.

The politics of feminism for the 99 percent

The preceding analysis informs the fundamental political point of our *Manifesto*: feminism must rise to the occasion of the current crisis. As we said, this is a crisis that capitalism can at best displace but cannot solve. A true resolution requires nothing less than an entirely new form of social organization.

Certainly, our *Manifesto* does not prescribe the precise contours of an alternative, as the latter must emerge in the course of the struggle to create it. But some things are already clear. Contra liberal feminism, sexism cannot be defeated by equal-opportunity domination—nor, contra ordinary liberalism, by legal reform. By the same token, and *pace* traditional understandings of socialism, an exclusive focus on wage labor's exploitation cannot emancipate women—nor, indeed, working people of any gender. It is also necessary to target capital's instrumentalization of unwaged reproductive labor, to which exploitation is in any case tied. What is needed, in fact, is to overcome the system's stubborn nexus of production and reproduction, its entwinement of profit-making with people-making, and its subordination of the second to the first. And this means abolishing the larger system that generates their symbiosis.

Our *Manifesto* identifies liberal feminism as a major obstacle to this emancipatory project. That current achieved its present dominance by outlasting, indeed reversing, the feminist radicalism of the previous period. The latter had arisen in the 1970s on the crest of a powerful wave of anti-colonial struggles against war, racism, and capitalism. Sharing in their revolutionary ethos, it questioned the entire structural basis of the existing order. But when the radicalism of that era subsided, what emerged as hegemonic was a feminism shorn of utopian, revolutionary aspirations—a feminism that reflected, and accommodated, mainstream liberal political culture.

Liberal feminism is not the whole story, of course.

Combative anti-racist and anticapitalist feminist currents have continued to exist. Black feminists have produced insightful analyses of the intersection of class exploitation, racism, and gender oppression, and newer materialist queer theories have disclosed important links between capitalism and the oppressive reification of sexual identities. Militant collectives have kept up their hard, day-to-day, grassroots work, and Marxist feminism is now undergoing a revival. Nevertheless, the rise of neoliberalism transformed the general context in which radical currents had to operate, weakening every pro–working class movement while empowering corporate-friendly alternatives—liberal feminism among them.

Today, however, liberal feminist hegemony has begun to crumble, and a new wave of feminist radicalism has emerged from the rubble. As we noted in our *Manifesto*, the key innovation of the current movement is the adoption and reinvention of the strike. By striking, feminists have taken a form of struggle identified with the workers' movement and retooled it. Withholding not only waged work, but also the unwaged work of social reproduction, they have disclosed *the latter's indispensable role in capitalist society*. Making visible women's power, they have challenged labor unions' claim to "own" the strike. Signaling their unwillingness to accept the existing order, feminist strikers are re-democratizing labor struggle, restating what should have been obvious: strikes belong to the working class *as a whole*—not to a partial stratum of it, nor to particular organizations.

The potential effects are very far-reaching. As we noted in our *Manifesto*, feminist strikes are forcing us to re-think what constitutes class and what counts as class struggle. Karl Marx famously theorized the working class as the "universal class." What he meant was that by fighting to overcome its own exploitation and domination, the working class was also challenging a social system that oppresses the overwhelming majority of the world's population and, thereby, forwarding the cause of humanity as such. But Marx's followers have not always grasped that neither the working class nor humanity is an undifferentiated, homogenous entity and that universality cannot be achieved by ignoring their internal differences. We are still paying the price today for these political and intellectual lapses. While neoliberals cynically celebrate "diversity" in order to prettify capital's predations, too many sections of the left still fall back on the old formula holding that what unites us is an abstract and homogenous notion of class, and that feminism and anti-racism can only divide us.

What is becoming increasingly clear, however, is that the standard portrait of the militant worker as

white and male is badly out of sync with the times—
indeed, it was never accurate in the first place. As
we argued in our *Manifesto*, today's global working class also comprises billions of women,
immigrants, and people of color. It struggles not
only in the workplace, but also around social
reproduction, from the food riots central to the
Arab revolutions, to the movements against
gentrification that occupied Istanbul's Taksim
Square, to the struggles against austerity and in
defense of social reproduction that animated the
Indignados.

Our *Manifesto* rejects both perspectives, the
class-reductionist left one that conceives the
working class as an empty, homogeneous
abstraction; and the progressive-neoliberal one
that celebrates diversity for its own sake. In their
place, we have proposed a universalism that
acquires its form and content from the multiplicity
of struggles from below. To be sure, the differences,
inequalities, and hierarchies that inhere in capitalist
social relations *do* give rise to conflicts of interest
among the oppressed and exploited. And by itself,
the proliferation of fragmentary struggles will not
give birth to the sort of robust, broad-based
alliances needed to transform society. However,
such alliances will become utterly impossible if we
fail to take our differences seriously. Far from

proposing to obliterate or trivialize them, our *Manifesto* advocates that we fight against capitalism's weaponization of our differences. Feminism for the 99 percent embodies this vision of universalism: always in formation, always open to transformation and contestation, and always establishing itself anew through solidarity.

Feminism for the 99 percent is a restless anticapitalist feminism—one that can never be satisfied with equivalences until we have equality, never satisfied with legal rights until we have justice, and never satisfied with democracy until individual freedom is calibrated on the basis of freedom for all.